Pain
Suffering
Hope

By Don Singer

PublishAmerica
Baltimore

First printing

At the specific preference of the author, PublishAmerica allowed this work to remain exactly as the author intended, verbatim, without editorial input.

ISBN: 1-4137-9486-6
PUBLISHED BY PUBLISHAMERICA, LLLP
www.publishamerica.com
Baltimore

Printed in the United States of America

I have felt pain
I have suffered
I have hope

Why I Hate You

I wake up longing for you.
My first thoughts are of you only.
I miss you more than life itself.
How can I live without you.

My boss calls am I coming to work?
No I'm sick today. But I'm not.
My wife calls, lunch today?
No I'm sick today. But I'm not.

My kids ask Dad do you want play ball?
No daddy is sick today. But I'm not.
The bills come due.
I say I'm too busy today. But I'm not.

You say what are you doing today.
I say waiting to spend it with you.
My life is nothing without you.
I hate you crack cocaine.

Lost In The Desert

I crawled in the woods as a baby.
I walked in the woods as a child.
I walked in the woods as a teenager.
I woke in the desert as a man.

How has this happened?
Where did I change?
What kind of a father am I?
I can't believe this has happened to me.

Help me please I can't stop this.
I don't want this anymore.
No more please.
What must I do to stop this?

Listen

Giving

I gave you my car.
You said I need more.
I gave you my boat.
You said I need more.

I gave you my house.
You said I need more.
I gave you my kids.
You said I need more.

I gave you me.
You said I need more.
I said all I have left is to suffer.
You said that's all I ever wanted.

Where are you?

I looked across the table
And couldn't see you.
I looked behind me
And couldn't see you.

I looked to my right
And couldn't see you.
I looked to my left
And couldn't see you.

I looked up
And couldn't see you.
I looked down
And couldn't see you.

I feel to my knees
And said
God where are you?
And a small voice said "Here"

Found

I was lost but now I'm found.
I'm glad it wasn't in the ground.
I was lost but now I'm found.
Even if it was in the dog pound.

I was lost but now I'm found
I'm glad I can still act like a clown
I was lost but now I'm found
I'm just glad I don't wear a frown.

I was lost but now I'm found
I know everyone thinks I'm a clown
I was lost but now I'm found
I'm sure glad I'm not fooling around.

I was lost but now I'm found
I'm Just Glad To Be

Life

I wake up it's raining.
Flowers need water
I wake up the wind is blowing
The yard is clean.

I wake up a tree is blown over.
I have firewood now.
I wake up the electricity is out.
My bill will be less this month.

I wake up there is no water.
I hate to bath everyday anyway.
I wake up someone has passed away.
I think of all the good things they did.

I wake up my legs are gone.
I have two arms and my mind.
I wake up.
I'm glad.

Call

I feel empty and alone
I feel abandon
I feel no one cares
My day begins

I don't know what the day will bring
Will I survive this day?
How many hills to climb today
How many valleys with no way out

The phone rings
My day is bright
To be needed,
Is to help someone

The Way Out

I became aware today
I'm a human being
I'm a child being taught
You gave me values and my life

Like a tree near water I grew
My roots were strong
And the ground was firm
I stood tall and proud

I said I don t need you
My roots are deep
So dry up you lazy stream
I have all I need without you

I turned my back to you
I no longer looked at you
And yet you still fed me
Even though I paid you no attention

Then came the storms
I new this was the end
The ground around my roots softened
The wind blew and over I went

My life is over
But wait can this be

Yes I feel so light
I feel new yes new
There are people playing on me
How can this be?

It was then the stream said
Your purpose has just begun.

Daddy

Daddy will you play a game with me
Yes I will but later OK.

Daddy can we go to the movies
Yes tomorrow we will go

Daddy will you come to my game tomorrow
Yes I will be there I promise

Daddy will you please make the next game
Yes I promise I will

Daddy this is the last game of the year
OK I'll be there I promise

Daddy do you love me
Yes I promise

Liar

No Sleep

Why can't I sleep?
Something is missing , I'm empty inside
I toss and turn all night
Why won't you shut up?

I can't do that, I can't do that
On and on my mind goes.
Who's there, who's not there
What's that stop that

I don't want to think about that
No! No! No! No!
Thank God It's morning
1A.M.6 hours to go

I finally sleep
What! It's 1:30 cold sweats
Was that real or a dream?
I can't do this

I want to write but I can't
I try to read but I can't
I grab a book and say
God help me please

I fall asleep
I wake to the alarm at 6:45
I look at the book in my Hands
The Good News

I now sleep well after
I say God help me at night
I Pick up The Good News
And go to sleep

?

What's wrong you look sad?
Nothing

Are you hungry?
No

Did someone hurt you today?
No

Did you have an accident?
No

You look angry are you mad at someone?
No

Are you sleeping, you look tired?
No

Is there anything you want?
Yes someone to talk to.

This Day

I wake up to the birds singing
The sky is a beautiful blue
I hear the waves on the beach
I look across the white sand
And see the waves crash on the beach
A child runs into the surf
Thank you Lord for this day

Things

I sit on the grass in the park
The squirrels are chasing each other
The sounds of birds come from the trees
In the sky I see the tail of a kite

The sound of a child kicking a ball
A mother sits on a blanket with her baby
While a toy boat sails by on the pond
I see a dog catch a Frisbee in flight

Eye

Eyes see a mother nursing a child
Eyes see a bird feeding her young
Eyes see lion cubs at play
Eyes see a pony running in a field

Eyes see a hawk circling above
Eyes see a salmon jump upstream
Eyes see a bear playing by the stream
I see my life, as I want it to be

What I found

I hear the water falling
I smell the flowers
I feel the water rushing
I see the beautiful colors

I hear the frogs calling
I smell the forest scent
I see a frog jump on a log
I want to show you what I found

You Must Be The Son

You must be the sun
Because I am the moon
And without you I don't shine.

I looked for you in my youth
And didn't see you

I looked for you in my work
And didn't see you

I looked for you in my wife
And didn't see you

I looked for you in my children
And didn't see you

I looked for you in a bottle
And lost myself

I turned to you
And now I shine

You

When I see a Sunset I see You
When I hear Birds I hear You
When I smell Flowers I smell You
When I feel Joy I Feel You
When I'm at Peace I've found You

Life Has Passed Me By

I look up at the sky as the clouds go by
Leaves float by from the trees above
A horse gallops by and into a stream
A fish swims by on his way the sea
I've learned to enjoy life passing me by.

Dream Come True

What a beautiful dream to dream of you
I turn to see my dream has come true.

Needs

I think of yesterday and cry
How can I ever repay you?
Then I realize you are still here
You will meet all my needs today

I have hope for a better tomorrow
I have your love to satisfy me
I know I can always turn to you
Whenever troubles come my way

Thank you for forgiveness
Thank you for understanding
Thank you for all I need
Thank you for my life

Starting My Day

I wake up at 5 o'clock
And look for you
I call to you
But there's no answer

I get on my knees
And pray you will forgive me
I ask you to protect me
And keep me safe

I begin this day
With all the hope and joy I can
I know what love is
And ask only for your will to be done.

If

What if I saw?
What if I felt
What if I could taste
What if I heard?
What if I could smell?
What if I just said I believe?

Smiles

Everyday has it's trials
Don't forget to says thanks with a smile

Remember when you woke this morning
Did you choose to start it mourning

I had yesterday
I have today
And will never have tomorrow.

Remember when you woke up
And said "Oh God it's morning"
Now it's thank you God for this morning.

I have a choice
Despair or repair

Crap rolls down hill
And makes valley green.

If wasn't for all the crap in my life
I wouldn't be the beautiful person I am today.
Modest too!

Change

Flowers need rain
Butterflies need caterpillars
Though you are in pain
I know you can change

Don't shut down and cry
Just give it a try
I tell you no lie
You can learn to fly

Just look inside
I know you're there
So give it a try
And learn to fly

Or don't your choice.

Rain

If it didn't rain
My windshield wipers would be useless
If it didn't rain
I could throw away my umbrella
If it didn't rain
No cutters would I need on my house?
If it didn't rain
No pump would I need in my basement?
If it didn't rain
There would be no water for fish
If it didn't rain
There would be no flowers
If it didn't rain
No life on the planet
THANK GOD IT'S RAINING

The only time I am unhappy
Is when I choose to be?
Make your choice today.

Garbage

Thank You
If it wasn't for you
I would have a kitchen full of garbage
If it wasn't for you
My trash cans would be full
If it wasn't for you
My driveway would be a mess
If it wasn't for you
My yard would be full of trash
If it wasn't for you
I just wouldn't know what do to
Thank you

If you don't take out the garbage
There'll be no room for the new stuff.
So thank you
Mr. Garbage Man

Shit Happens

When I stop playing the victim
Shit happens
When I stop feeling sorry for myself
Shit happens

When I take responsibility for my actions
Shit happens
When I stop complaining
Shit happens

When I accept everything
Shit happens
When I realize it's not about me
Life happens

Be

All my life I looked
All my life I was alone
I never seemed to be able to Be
I always needed to have

When all I ever wanted was to just Be
Today I can just sit and Be
To be comfortable with me
And not feel alone

To like myself
To spend time with myself
To be responsible for what I do
To be responsible for what I don't do

A great peace can be found in the truth
No more lies
No more stories
What a joy it is to Be

What Good

Why do people have to suffer
What good can come from that

Why did I have to drink so must
What good can come from that

Why did I have to ruin my life
What good can come from that

Why did I have to wind up in the hospital
What good can come from that

Why did I have to go thru all that
What good can come from all that

Why do I have to tell somebody else my story
What good can come from that

Why me
To Help You

If you still don't get it
Just help the guy next to you

Which One Do You Find

I find anger when I look for it
I find peace when I look for it

I find suffering when I look for it
I find happiness when I look for it

I find sadness when I look for it
I find joy when I look for it

I find hate when I look for it
I find love when I look for it

What do you find when you look?
I find a choice which one do you choose?

If I only do one thing today
Let it be the right one

Inside

There are two groups
One side says go ahead
The other side says no don't
You know a tug of war

Only my brain is gona tear apart
And I just can't seem to stop this war
I scream shut up but they still argue
I just need a little to settle my nerves

I can't take this anymore
You just don't understand what it's like
This battle in my head that won't stop
If I just have one little one

How did, Why did, How could I,
When will I, I'll never be able to stop
God help me to change
I thought you'd never ask.

Fright

Today I woke up with a fright
What will I do today
I just don't want to get out of bed
I don't want to hear today's troubles
Is everyone ok, who cares
I fear the day ahead
Will I make it thru the day
I don't want to call anyone
I don't want to see anyone
If only the noise would stop
Please shut up I can't take this
As I fall to my knees and say God help me
My head starts to clear and I relax
I can enjoy this day
That's right every time I help someone
I seem to feel better let me call someone
Better yet let me go help someone
Lord as always your will be done not mine

The Sculptor

First a sculptor sees the beauty in a rock
Then he removes all the waste around it

God is at work on you right now
Some of us need more hammering than others

This day must end before a new one begins

If I think long enough
About why I should not do something

Then I'll find the only reason
Why I should

Searching

I feel empty and alone inside
I'm searching and can't find it
I fill my time with sports
Still I can't find it

I fill my time with people
Still I can't find it
I fill my time with drinking
And no longer feel alone

I feel empty and alone inside
Still I can't find it
I fill my time with drinking
And no longer feel alone

I feel empty and alone inside
Still I can't find it
I fill my time with drinking
And want to be left alone

I feel empty and alone inside
Still I can't find it
I fill my time with drinking
I no longer feel and I no longer am

I feel empty and alone inside
Still I can't find it
I fill my time with drinking
???

I feel empty and alone inside
Still I can't find it
I fill my time with drinking
???

I feel empty and alone inside
Still I can't find it
I fill my time with drinking
???

Will this ever end
Maybe I can make this end
A knife, a bullet, poison
A rope, a cliff

What?
I don't
And people say I'm crazy
Do you know who I am !

Wind

I look into your eyes
And see the ocean

I touch your hands
And feel relief

I run my hands through your hair
And feel the wind

Fear

Why am I afraid
What am I afraid of
Who am I afraid of

My stomach hurts
My head hurts
I want this to stop

I don't care
Leave me alone
You don't understand

Please I can't stand this
Why can't I tell you
Why can't I ask you

I need you but can't ask
Please help me
Please ask me

Do you

Do you understand me
Can you feel what's wrong
Do you know the loneliness
Can you feel my pain

Do you live in fear
Can you feel my suffering
Do you know what I mean
Can you tell someone for me

Do you know what the difference
Between you and me is
Communication

Life is like a well-rounded meal
If you eat right
Life's shit is easy to take

If you don't fill your mind with good thoughts
It will be empty when you need one

If you want a light hearted journey
Leave your baggage behind

If you don't want bugs
Throw out the garbage

Put your right foot forward
And forget what you left behind

If I leave my glasses on the floor
Who do I blame when they get broken

Surrender to win

You cannot be born again
Until you first die

So put your old self to death
So you can be born again

Are you afraid to enjoy life
Are you afraid to be happy

Then be sad, be in pain
I was there and now I'm not

It's not the miles
But the roads we travel

If you traveled the same roads I have
You know the pain
If you are traveling the roads I traveled
You are feeling the pain
Don't give up lookup

As I

As I opened my eyes
I thought of the coming day
As I opened my eyes
I felt despair

As I sat up in bed
I thought how can I face this day
As I sat up in bed
I felt I needed help

As I slid to my knees
I thought how will this help
As I slid to my knees
I felt a little foolish

As I knelt by my bed
I thought what should I say
As I knelt by my bed
I felt it was OK

As I folded my hands
I started to pray
As I folded my hands
I knew I would be OK

I Hurt

I wake up and wish I hadn't
What's wrong with me
I don't deserve to be alive
What's wrong with me

Due I have to go on living like this
What's wrong with me
I hate my life
What's wrong with me

I hate to look at myself
What's wrong with me
If you knew how I feel
What's wrong with me

I can't believe this is normal
What's wrong with me
This noise won't stop
What's wrong with me

I can't stop the voices
What's wrong with me
I just want to sleep
What's wrong with me

Look At Me

I am 25 years old
You are 75 years old

I am smooth skinned and tan
You are wrinkled and pale

I walk tall and proud
You walk bent over and use a cane

I don't need anyone
You need everyone

I feel alone in a crowd
You are at home in a crowd

I don't like people who don't like me
You say it's ok if people don't like you

I think I know why I like you
You look at me not around me

Thank you for looking at me

Just A Bird

What's that noise
It's Just A Bird
Oh 5 o'clock I've got to get up
It's Just A Bird

I go to the window
It's Just A Bird
I see a shadow move
It's Just A Bird

What's that moving
It's Just A Bird
Now I see it
It's Just A Brown Bird

No that's not right
It's Just A Red Bird
No it's a Blue Bird
Does it matter thank you God

The Same

It's a different day
I feel the same
I checked the calendar
I feel the same

I know it's today
I feel the same
It's not yesterday
I feel the same

Tomorrow isn't here yet
I feel the same
Can this be true
I feel the same

I never thought
I could feel the same
It's OK today
To feel the same

Did you

Did you ever wakeup
And not want to
Did you ever wakeup
AND NOT WANT TO

Did you ever wakeup alone
And not want to
Did you ever wakeup alone
AND NOT WANT TO

Did you ever wakeup blind
And not want to
Did you ever wakeup blind
AND NOT WANT TO

Did you ever wakeup dying
And not want to
Did you ever wakeup dying
AND NOT WANT TO

Wakeup before you don't

Cake

Have you ever baked a cake
You need all the ingredients
What happens if you leave one out
You need all the ingredients

Did you ever eat some cake
You need all the ingredients
How did it taste when something was missing
You need all the ingredients

Can you imagine a world
You need all the ingredients
With one kind of person
You need all the ingredients

When you next meet someone
You need all the ingredients
Ask them about all their ingredients
Hope you liked this cake

Take A Look

Do you think I'm crazy
Or are you the crazy one
Do you think I'm stupid
Or are you the stupid one

Am I the smart one
Or are you the smart one
Did I want to write this
Or did you want this written

Was I afraid to write this
Or were you afraid to read this
Do I know why I wrote this
Or do you know why you're reading this

I wrote this for you
You are reading this for me
I wrote this for me
You are reading this for you

Thank you for reading this
Now we are we

How Can I Tell You

I can't help you
I want so much to help
I don't know how
What can I do
If I call no one answers
If I write no one reads
People will think I'm crazy
People will get mad at me
I will be so embarrassed
Everyone will then know
He's a sick person
How can I tell you
The loneliness I feel
How can I tell you
The shame I feel
How can I tell you
Will you listen
I just told you

Missing

What am I missing
I have food to eat
What am I missing
I have clothes to wear
What am I missing
I have my health
What am I missing
My family is in good health
What am I missing
I have a place to live
What am I missing
I have taken care of everything
What am I missing
The point

Watching

Do you see the egg
How long before the bird
Do you see the seed
How long before the flower
Do you see the caterpillar
How long before the butterfly
Do you see the rain
How long before the sunshine
Do you see the hurt
How long before you help\
Do you feel the pain
How long before you ask
Do you want to change
How long before you are willing

What Did I Find

What did I find when I wrote this
I found my voice

What did I find
I found help

What did I find
I found you

What did I find
My healing

What did I find
I found me

Please talk to someone
Then you too can find yourself

And find peace

God Bless and comfort you

The Pain was the way I felt many days in my life.

The Suffering was what I did to get by in life.

The Hope is that this will touch you enough to pass this along to someone else who might also be lost at the moment.

Miracles really do happen. Just look around you will see them everywhere. The trick is YOU have to want to see them.

I know some of what you just read was not anything new. For most of my life I felt like a tapestry on the wall. I just never felt comfortable in a room or crowd. Always I felt like people were watching me and that made me nervous. Now if you can relate to this I know you feel what I felt then. Today it's OK to be the tapestry on the wall. At least for me it is. I don't have to escape to be accepted. I no longer need to pour something down my throat, inhale something into my lungs, inject something into my blood, or take a pill. Shit used to happen to me but today life happens.

A Tapestry can be a beautiful thing and today I am part of the tapestry.